The Little Cézanne

Catherine de Duve

Discover Provence and Paris with the father of Cubism

KATE'ART EDITIONS

CÉZANNE'S

From here I have an interesting view, blue sky, red roofs... It's perfect! To work!

All is calm in this village in Provence. Gardanne stands on the hill, facing Mont Sainte-Victoire. The red-roofed houses tumble down towards the plain. The bell tower dominates the small mining town. In the shadow of a plane tree, Cézanne searches for a view that can inspire him. Easel, canvas, paintbrushes and paints on his back, he goes down small alleyways. The painter settle down to paint. Cézanne loves to paint outdoors, directly from nature. It was this new method that revolutionised painting.

PROVENCE

Cézanne is a native of this land. He loves his Provence, its light, colours, fragrance, dry scrubland, rosemary, pine trees, rocks, hills, mountains and its beautiful blue sky!

He works tirelessly to explore the secrets of the landscape's shapes and colours.

🔍 Discover the Provence Cézanne knew.

Mont Sainte-Victoire

The blocks of stone from the Bibémus quarry

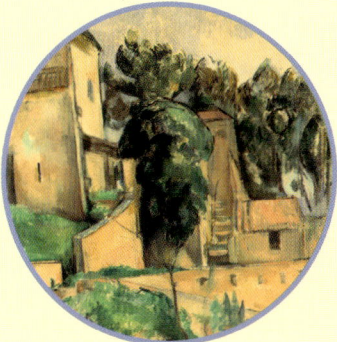

The Provençal villages

The fishing village of Estaque

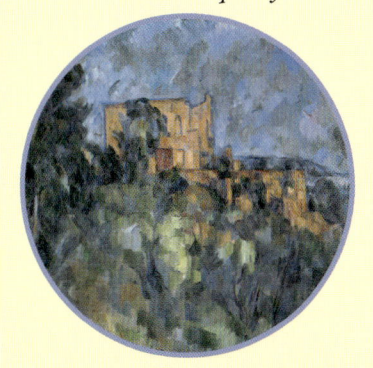

The mysterious Black Castle

The forests of the Black Castle

The Jas de Bouffan, the family home

PAUL CÉZANNE

Imagine a story that begins: "On the way back from the river..." and draw what happens.

Paul Cézanne was born in Aix-en-Provence in southern France on the 19th of January 1839. His parents, Louis-Auguste and Anne Elizabeth Honorine were not yet married, but soon their family was beginning to grow! Paul has two sisters, Mary and Rose. His father was a modest seller and exporter of hats, but he later becomes a banker and a wealthy man.

At School...

One day in the playground Cézanne defends a not very strong, short-sighted boy from bullies. The little boy is Émile Zola who will one day become a great French writer. The next day Zola brings him a basket of apples. It's the start of a great friendship! The two friends become inseparable. They love exploring the Provencal countryside, fishing and swimming in the little river Arc.

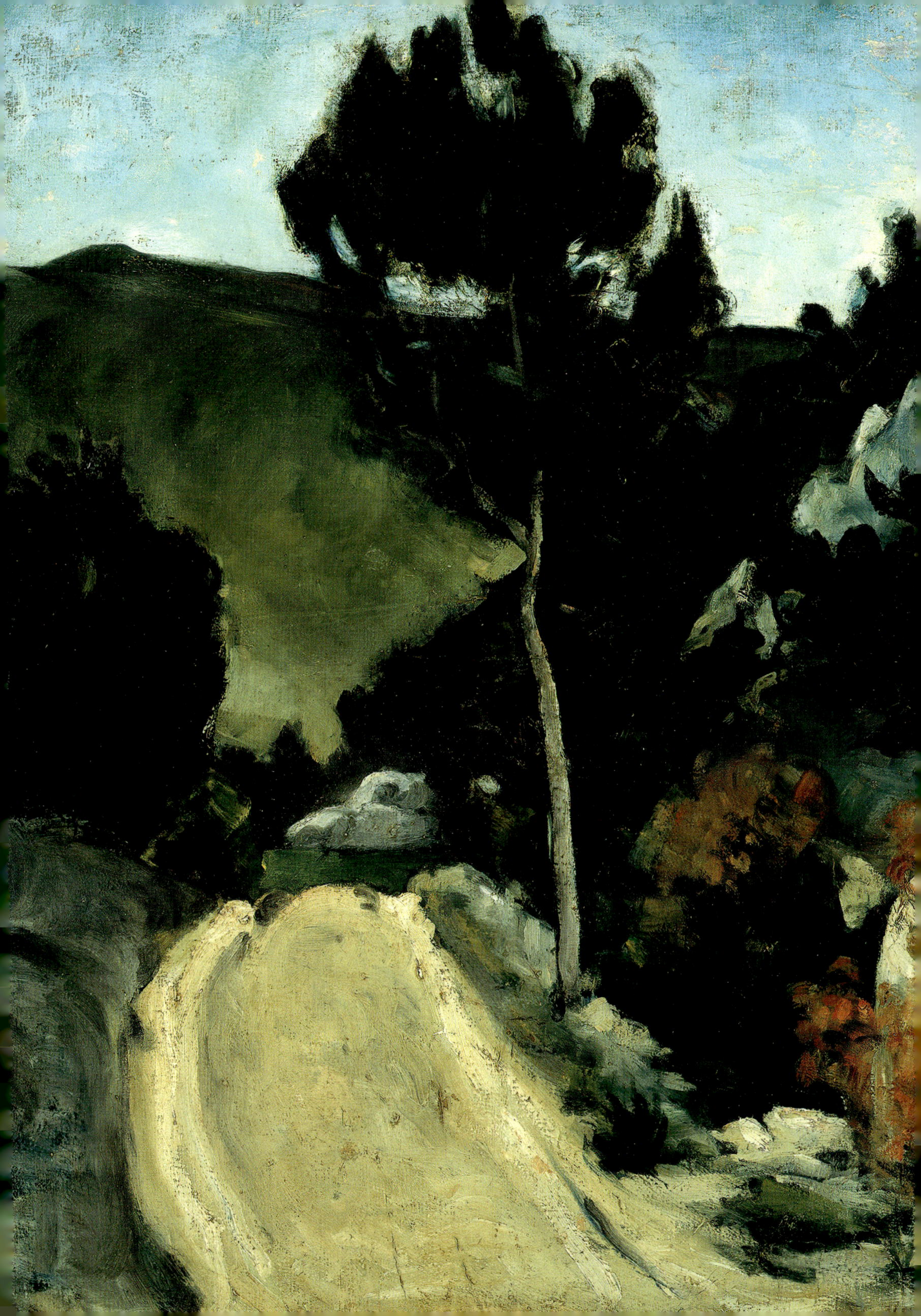

SEE YOU IN PARIS!

In 1858 Cézanne's best-friend Zola leaves for Paris. He wants to try his luck as a writer. The two friends write long letters to each other. However, Cézanne's father wants him to become a banker! Resigned to his father's wishes, Paul studies law at the University of Aix, but in the evening he also goes to drawing classes.

Two years later Cézanne goes to Paris. His father agrees to let him follow his own path. Finally! He studies at the Swiss Academy where he meets Pissarro, Monet and Renoir. He goes to the Louvre and copies the masterpieces of Titian, Rubens and Michelangelo. He also discovers the work of Delacroix and admires his use of colour. Despite his best efforts, he is rejected by the School of Fine Arts.

Here is his copy of a painting by Delacroix. Look at how Cézanne uses colour to create sculptural forms.

Cézanne feels like a stranger in Paris despite the artistic energy and buzz of the city. They make fun of his rough accent and his provincial manners. He is uncomfortable among the bourgeoisie and prefers to be alone. He is seen as an eccentric.

Who is this character? What is he wearing? In your opinion what is his job?

● Painter ● Banker ● Gardener ● Writer ● Priest ● Lawyer

THE RECLUSE OF AIX

He becomes homesick and makes many journeys back and forth to Aix. He never stays more than six consecutive months in Paris. When he is in Paris he takes the opportunity to present his paintings to the official Salon. They are always rejected, but he does not take the rejection to heart.

Cézanne spreads his paint heavily with a palette knife.

HORTENSE

In 1869, during one of his stays in Paris, Cézanne meets Hortense Fiquet. She works as a model. They soon decide to live together. Cézanne has to hide this relationship from his father. He is scared that he'll be cut off financially if his father learns about it...

In general, Cézanne avoids contact with women who intimidate him. With Hortense it is different, he feels good. She poses for him and he paints forty portraits of her. Here she is looking serious. Is she bored?

It's so hot in the greenhouse! How is Hortense dressed? Her body is hidden under an imposing black dress, buttoned up tight to the neck. It looks as if he has painted her dress as if it were a mountain! Hortense is very patient and keeps the same pose for many hours. After all, it's her job.

🔍 Look at the hands of Hortense. We can only see the tips of her fingers. She is wearing delicate mittens.

🔍 What plants are growing in the greenhouse?

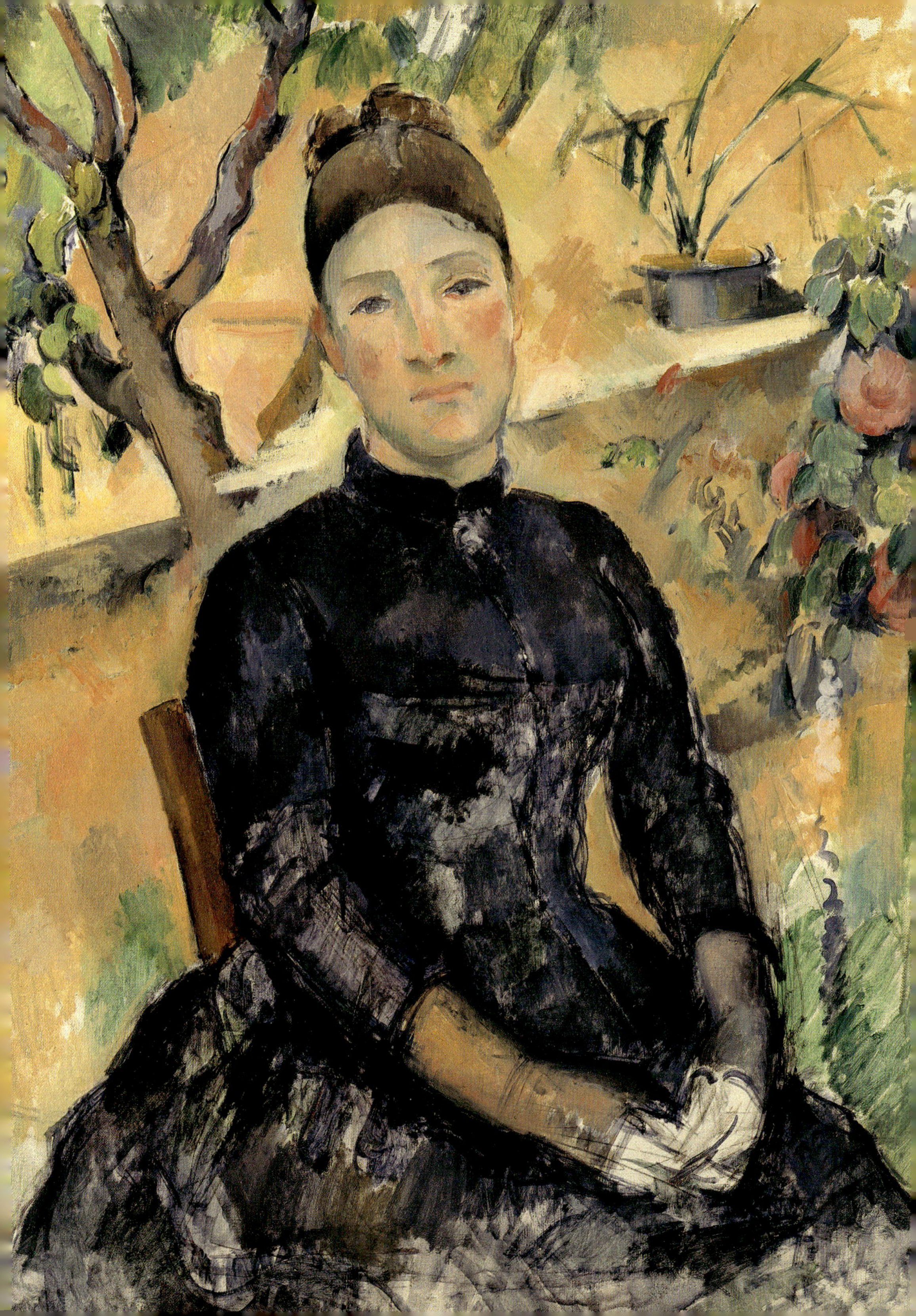

ESTAQUE

In 1870 war breaks out between France and Prussia (now part of Germany). Cézanne and Hortense take refuge in Estaque, a small fishing village near Marseilles. This way the painter escapes being called up to the army. He does not want to fight!

Cézanne is fascinated by the Mediterranean landscape. The blue sky contrasts beautifully with the jagged white rocks. The dry, cracked red earth and the sea, the pine and emerald green olive trees, the landscape is full of contrast!

Cézanne returns to Estaque later in his life and paints the Gulf of Marseilles.

🔍 Find the geometric shapes in the painting.

Cézanne goes back to his paintings and makes changes to them.
He has very high standards. He even destroys some paintings when he's not satisfied. What a perfectionist!

How are the walls and red roofs of the houses transformed into geometric shapes by Cézanne's brush?

The trees become spheres, houses become cubes, and hills turn into trapeziums...

Draw a Mediterranean landscape in the style of Cézanne.

A LESSON IN IMPRESSIONISM

After the end of the war Hortense and Cézanne return to Paris. It is in Paris that their son Paul is born in 1872. Soon his friend and fellow painter Camille Pissarro invites Paul to join him in the Oise valley near Auvers-sur-Oise, a small town close to Paris. Here he meets Dr. Gachet, an amateur painter and art collector. He was to be Cézanne's first customer.

Cézanne displays his work at Impressionist exhibitions but he quickly distanced himself from the movement. Instead he steps up his efforts to be on show at the official Salon, which still does not accept his or the Impressionists' work.

Pissarro was like a father to me, a little like God.

Pissarro believes Cézanne to be exceptionally talented and introduces him to Impressionist techniques and painting outdoors, "en plein air". Soft colours are applied in small brush strokes.

Look at the Impressionist brush strokes of Cézanne. How does this picture make you feel?

JAS DE BOUFFAN

The wind picks up at Jas de Bouffan... In 1859 Cézanne's father buys this house. It is the old summer residence of the Governor of Provence, the *Jas* de Bouffan, west of Aix. What a strange name! It means "House of the Wind."

Aged 20, Cézanne, with his father's permission, decorates the walls of the living room with large murals depicting the Four Seasons. Cézanne enjoys his work there and becomes very fond of the building.

Jas is the Provençal word for "shelter". These are large sheep barns built with dry stone (without mortar) surrounded by grazing pastures away from the farm and village.

It's winter. Bare trees provide clean lines for the painter to draw. The pool of water reflects the sky and buildings, but also leaves a remarkable emptiness. Cézanne follows his instincts as he paints.
He increasingly simplifies his compositions. He wants to show the essence of the scene. No frills, no decorative effect... Everything is stripped bare.

Find the Jas de Bouffan in different seasons.
Look at the change in Cézanne's technique.
In your opinion, what order were these paintings created in?

APPLES!

I want to conquer Paris with an apple!

Cézanne reinvents an old and very traditional genre: still life. He chooses round and colourful fruits as his subjects. Juicy cherries, rosy, red apples, green pears and yellow peaches. He adds dishes to the composition: a fruit bowl, a milk jug, a vase of flowers, an earthenware dish and a ginger jar... Each one is positioned carefully on the table.

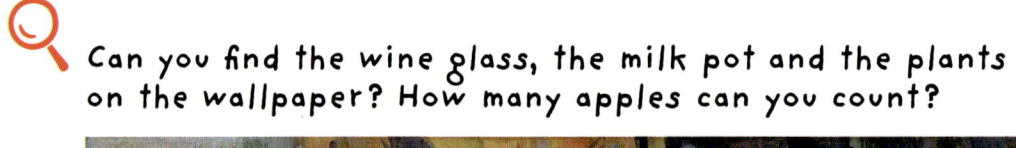

🔍 Can you find the wine glass, the milk pot and the plants on the wallpaper? How many apples can you count?

Often Cézanne adds a carefully unfolded white tablecloth. How strange! It's as if you can see the table from the front and from above at the same time.

Cézanne works hard to paint objects from several different perspectives. The front of the table is painted as if we were facing it. It seems to be our height. This is the front perspective. But at the same time it's also possible to see the whole platter as if we were looking down on it from above. That's the raised perspective.

What is Cézanne trying to do by painting objects as if they were being viewed from different angles? Is he trying to emphasise their volume, their three-dimensional nature, or just to paint them as they really are?

It's your turn. Draw an object from a raised perspective, from the side and from the back, in the same drawing.

CARD PLAYERS

Cézanne works slowly. For his models the hours spent posing are endless. Hortense, who in the meantime has become his wife, and their son Paul are very patient. He also paints self-portraits. But Cézanne finds it more convenient and enjoyable to paint a landscape or a still life. At least those subjects stay still!

Who else models for him? Farmers and labourers who work in the fields of Jas de Bouffan come to pose for him for a little money. Can you see the man smoking his pipe? It's Alexandre, the gardener of the household.

Where does this scene take place? Find these details in the painting.

The card players have curved shoulders due to the hard, manual work they have to do during the day. The evening is the time to finally relax by playing cards. Their hands and faces are coloured orange to show their concentration.
Their faces give off no emotion. Are they wearing their overalls? Which of the two is better at the game?

MONT SAINTE-VICTOIRE

In 1897, after the death of their mother, Cézanne and his two sisters decide to sell Jas de Bouffan. It's a sad decision for the painter.
A few years later, in 1901, he buys a small house in the hills around Lauves where he sets up his own studio. From there he sees the Sainte-Victoire Mountain. The mystery that surrounds it fascinates Cézanne.
How should he paint it?

Look at the details of the picture. Find the essential elements of the landscape: the trees, the rocks, the mountain and the house.

Cézanne is trying to create something as beautiful and lasting as "the art in museums".

Trees, fields and houses form a mosaic. It's impossible to identify them all individually. It is through seeing them all together that the subject of the painting appears. His touches of colour fragment reality and reconstruct the landscape. It's the genius of Cézanne! His strokes are carefully sculpted and give the painting depth. The cool blue of the mountain emphasises its distance, whereas the warm ochre of the Provencal plains brings them closer to the viewer.

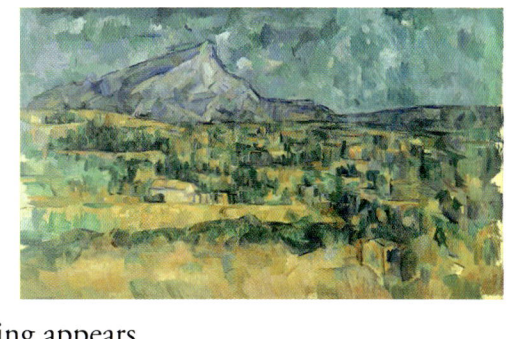

STUDIO

🔍 **Look at the colour of the sun-scorched stone.**

During his life Cézanne has several different workshops. Here he stores his equipment and tirelessly edits his pictures which he often paints outside in nature.

His father arranges a small studio for him under the roof of Jas de Bouffan. Cézanne works there continuously until the sale of the family home. He then moves into an apartment on Boulegon Street, in central Aix, not far from the Cézanne family bank! To store his equipment Cézanne rents a cottage in the maze of ochre limestone rocks at the Bibémus quarry. From the terrace he can see Mont Sainte-Victoire.

The painter also rents a room in the Black Castle, on the road to his favourite mountain. Can you see how the walls have turned red? He tries to buy it, but without success. He then buys land on the hill and builds his new house there in Lauves. On the first floor he builds a beautiful studio with a large glass window.
He cuts a slot in the wall large enough to pass large canvases through, and uses this for example, for "The Bathers". Can you see him posing for the photograph?

🔍 Write a story about what happens at the Black Castle...

THE BATHERS

How many bathers can you count? Which ones are in the shape of trees? Find the dog.

At 60 years old the painter remembers the hours he once spent at the riverside. He fixes these happy memories of carelessness and joy in drawings, watercolours and oil paintings. He calls them "The Bathers". He creates huge paintings!

In a forest, the characters seem to be emerging from the water. Cézanne expresses his vision of a new Arcadia, the name of this imagined, happy and peaceful country. He wants to unite man and nature. The ochre and orange bodies of the bathers are as solid as the tree trunks they sit upon. The trees form a canopy that protects them. The scene is shot through with a blue which creates a dreamlike harmony. A dog sleeps quietly. Can you see him?

THE GARDENER

The portrait of Vallier the gardener is done in a few dynamic brush strokes. What can we see in the background? We cannot distinguish everything clearly. Everything seems to be sketched quickly. However, Cézanne has taken years to create this painting. And yet we cannot tell whether it's really finished… It is one of his last works.

His technique here is almost abstract. Can you tell what these details are intended to represent? Find them in the painting.

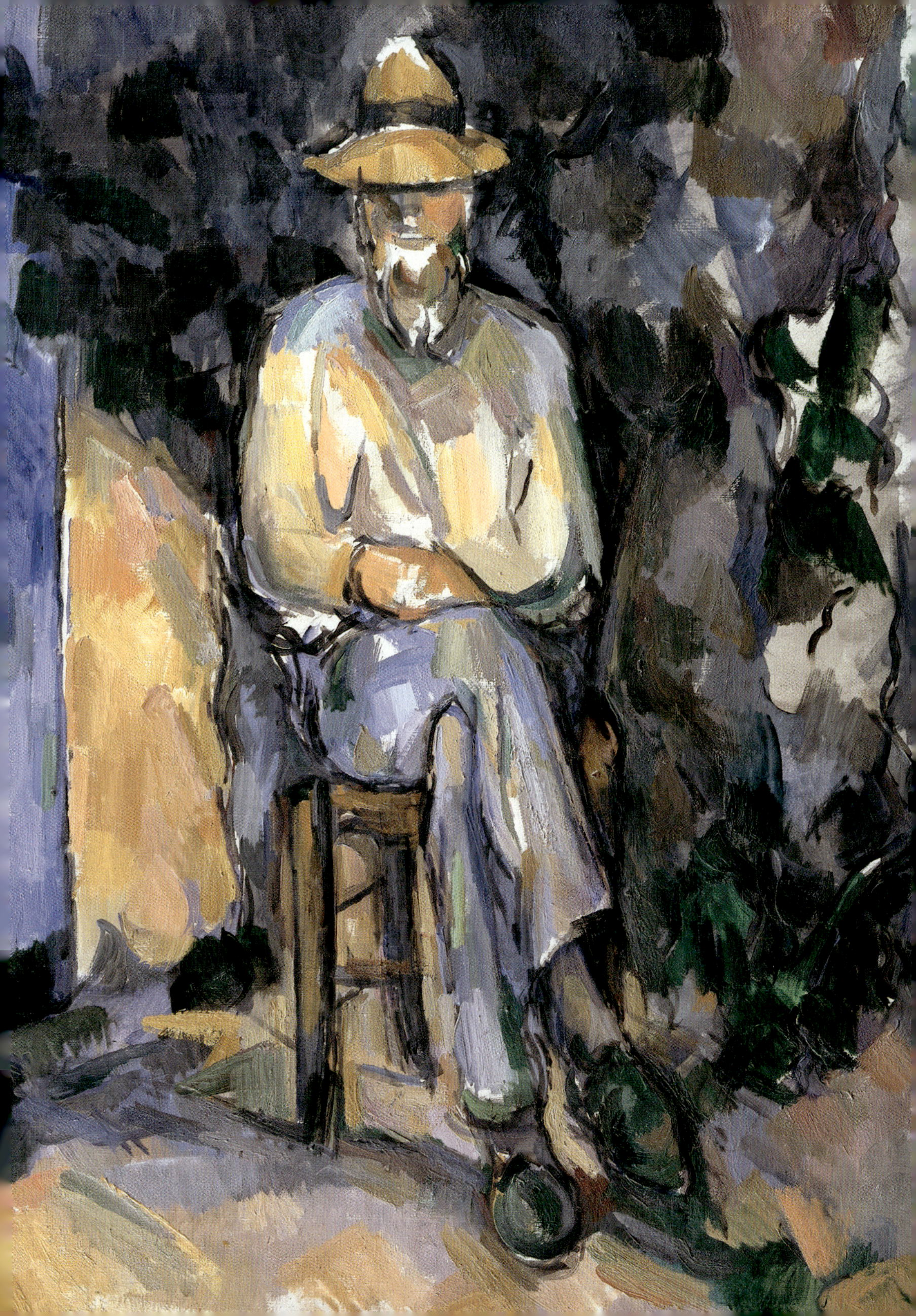

THE FIRST CUBIST!

Treat nature like a cylinder, a sphere, a cone... For Cézanne, nature has a depth and meaning beyond surface value. So there's a need to introduce light, new perspectives and life into his work, represented by red, yellow and a sufficient amount of blue "to enable the viewer to feel the air" as he writes in April 1904 in a letter to his friend, the painter Émile Bernard.

🔍 **What does this painting represent? Is it finished?**

Cézanne shows young, up-and-coming artists the way towards Cubism. Pablo Picasso called him "the father of us all". From now on he paints objects from many views at once. This includes views that are hidden when the viewer looks at an object. Geometric shapes start to appear...

Become a cubist painter! Use spheres, cubes, cones and cylinders to create a landscape.

SUCCESS FOR CÉZANNE!

During his career Cézanne is repeatedly misunderstood by the public. His technical innovations are very complex. Few people recognise his talent. But his time will come, Ambroise Vollard, the art dealer, organises an exhibition. He finally becomes successful!
A group of collectors, which includes Gertrude Stein, becomes increasingly interested in "the eccentric from Aix".

After this Cézanne displays his work in many exhibitions. His fame grows beyond France, reaching Berlin, Vienna and Brussels...

In 1900 he sends paintings to the Salon and the World Exhibition. Finally, in 1904, he succeeds. The Autumn Salon devotes a whole room to his work, where he displays 33 paintings. Hooray!

On October the 15th 1906, in the middle of autumn, a violent thunderstorm strikes. Cézanne is caught out in the storm. He stays outside in the pouring rain and cold for several hours. Finally a cart passes by and picks up the old painter. Back home, Cézanne is very weak...

He goes out one last time to his garden to make small changes to the portrait of his gardener Vallier before dying of pneumonia a few days later on October the 22nd, aged 67.

Text: Catherine de Duve
Research: Frédérique Masquelier
Concept and Production: Kate'Art Editions
Translation from the French: Stuart Forward

Photography credits:
Paris: Musée d'Orsay: *Self Portrait with a pink background* c. 1875: p. 1, p. 4 – *Uncle Dominique (the Lawyer)*, 1866: p. 7 – *The card players*, 1890-1899: cover, p. 18, p. 19 – *Still life with tureen, soupière*, cover, p. 4 | Musée Picasso: *Château Noir*, 1900-1904: p. 3, p. 23 | **London:** Tate Gallery: *The Gardener Vallier*, 1905-1906: p. 26-27 | The National Gallery: *Bathers*, 1894-1905: cover, p. 24-25 – *In the park of Château Noir*, c.1900-1904: cover, p. 3 | **Essen:** Museum Folkwang: *Bibemus quarry*, 1895: p. 3, p. 22 | **Baden:** Museum Langmatt, Stiftung Langmatt Sydney and Jenny Brown: *Trees and rocks in the park of the Château Noir*: cover, p. 3 | **Geneva:** Musées d'art et d'histoire de la ville de Genève: *The House at Bellevue*, c. 1890: p. 3, p. 30 | **Saint Petersburg:** Hermitage Museum: *Mont Sainte-Victoire, above the Tholonet road*, 1896-1898: p. 20 | **Cleveland:** The Cleveland Museum of Art: *Mont Sainte-Victoire, above the Tholonet road*, c. 1904: cover, p. 3, p. 21 | **Montreal:** Museum of Fine Arts: *Bend in a Road in Provence*, c. 1866: p. 4, p. 5 | **Washington, D.C.:** The Phillips Collection: *The Garden at Les Lauves*, c. 1906: p. 28 | National Gallery of Art: *Still Life with Milk Jug and Fruit*, c.1900: p. 16 - *House of Père Lacroix*, 1873: p. 12, p. 13 | **New-York:** The Metropolitan Museum of Art: *Madame Cézanne (née Hortense Fiquet, 1850 – 1922) in the Conservatory*, 1891-1892: cover, pp.8-9 – *The Gulf of Marseilles Seen from L'Estaque*, c.1885: p. 3, p. 10 – *Mont Sainte-Victoire*, c.1902-1906: p. 21 | Brooklyn Museum: *Gardanne*, c.1886: p. 2 | **Private collection:** *House with a red roof (Jas de Bouffan)*, 1885-1886: cover, p. 1, p. 14 – *The Barque of Dante (after Delacroix)*: p. 6 – *Basin of Jas de Bouffan in winter*, c. 1878: p. 15 | **Photographs:** *Cézanne*, 1889: p. 2, p. 13 – *Cézanne painting the Apotheosis of Delacroix*, 1894: p. 16 – Émile Bernard: *Cézanne in his studio at les Lauves, in front of* The Bathers, 1904: p. 23 – Kerr-Xavier Roussel: *Cézanne painting at les Lauves*, c.1906: p. 31

Thanks to: Frédérique Masquelier, Stuart Forward, Isabelle Gérard, Véronique Lux, Daniel de Duve, Valérie et Damien de Halleux and all those who contributed to the creation of this book.

The books of Kate'Art Editions are available in a variety of languages: French, English, Dutch, Spanish, German, Russian, Japanese and Danish.

Visit our online shop: *www.kateart.com*